CONTENTS

PREFACE

The work of a Magistrate is often misunderstood. It is viewed from a distance shaped by headlines, dramatized portrayals, or assumptions about the courtroom itself. Yet the true reality of magistracy is far quieter, far more human, and far more complex than many imagine. It is a role rooted not in authority for its own sake, but in service, fairness, and an unwavering responsibility to uphold the law while recognising the people behind it.

This book was written to offer an honest and accessible perspective on that world. It reflects the lessons learned during my years on the bench, the insights gained from countless cases, and the profound understanding that justice, at its core, is a human endeavour. It is influenced not only by my judicial experience but also by my later work in addiction, mental health, coaching, and behavioural change fields that revealed the deeper forces shaping the lives of many who enter the courtroom.

Balancing Justice is not a legal textbook, nor is it a sensationalised account of crime. It is a reflection on people: their vulnerabilities, their strengths, their mistakes, and their potential. It is a reminder that the courtroom is not merely a place of consequences, but a place of learning, accountability, and at its best transformation.

I hope that this book provides readers with a clearer understanding of what justice looks like from the inside: measured, thoughtful, compassionate, and firmly rooted in fairness. I hope it encourages reflection on how society responds to harm, how we support those in crisis, and how we might prevent many of the issues that lead people to court in the first place.

Above all, I hope it reinforces a simple truth: justice is not only about the law; it is about people.

DEDICATION

ACKNOWLEDGEMENTS

I would like to express my sincere gratitude to all those who supported me throughout my years of service in the magistracy and the work that followed.

To my colleagues on the bench thank you for your wisdom, your professionalism, and your shared commitment to fairness.

Serving alongside individuals who carried the same sense of duty and humility was a privilege.

To the legal advisors, clerks, ushers, probation officers, and support staff who keep the courts functioning your dedication often goes unnoticed by the public, but never by those who serve with you. You ensure that justice is not only delivered, but delivered with clarity and respect.

To those working in addiction services, mental health care, social support, and community organisations your work sits quietly at the intersection of justice and rehabilitation. I have seen firsthand the difference you make.

To my family thank you for your understanding and encouragement during the many years when my work involved difficult stories and long days. Your grounding presence made all the difference.

Finally, to every person who stood before the court thank you for the lessons you taught me. Your stories shaped my understanding of justice far more than any textbook or training ever could.

FOREWORD

The courtroom is a place where society's most pressing issues converge: addiction, mental illness, poverty, impulsive behaviour, fractured relationships, and lives under pressure.

It is also a place where fairness, accountability, and human dignity must coexist if justice is to be delivered in a meaningful way.

In *Balancing Justice*, Seán O'Connor offers a rare and valuable perspective on this world. Drawing on his years of experience as a Magistrate, alongside extensive work in behavioural change, addiction, mental health, and coaching, he provides an honest, compassionate, and deeply insightful account of what truly happens inside the courtroom.

This is not a book about legal procedure. It is a book about people the individuals who appear before the bench, the circumstances that shape their decisions, and the broader societal issues that drive much of the offending seen in our communities. With clarity and humility, Seán illustrates how justice must balance consequences with understanding, and how effective decision-making requires seeing beyond the offence to the person behind it.

What makes this book unique is not only the author's judicial experience, but the breadth of professional expertise he brings to interpreting human behaviour. Seán writes with both authority and empathy, revealing a justice system that is far more complex, nuanced, and human than many realise.

At a time when public debate about crime, punishment, and rehabilitation is more polarised than ever, this book offers something rare: perspective. Thoughtful, informed, balanced perspective. It reminds us that justice is not served solely by punishment, but by understanding, accountability, and the belief that people can change with the right support.

Balancing Justice is a valuable contribution to the conversation about fairness, responsibility, and the future of our justice system. It is a book that invites us to look beyond assumptions and to consider what justice really means not only in law, but in society.

Introduction

Sitting down to write this book, I find myself returning to the moment I first stepped onto the bench as a newly appointed Magistrate. It was a role steeped in tradition, responsibility, and public expectation, yet nothing can truly prepare you for the weight of dispensing justice on behalf of the community. The courtroom, with its rituals and its quiet intensity, would become a place where I witnessed humanity at its best, its worst, and everything in between. It was here that I learned not only about the law, but about the people it serves and sometimes fails.

My journey to that chair did not begin in a law library nor in a courtroom gallery.

It began in a working-class family in the North of England, where discipline, fairness, and service to others were not philosophical ideals but practical necessities. Those early years shaped much of who I became: someone who believed in second chances, in accountability, and in the profound impact that a single decision can have on a life.

When I was appointed as a Magistrate, I carried those values with me. What I did not yet appreciate was just how deeply the role would affect me how many stories I would encounter, how many difficult judgements I would have to make, and how often I would walk out of court reflecting on the complexity of human behaviour. The seat of a Magistrate is not elevated because one is superior; it is elevated so that one may see further beyond the offence, into the circumstances, vulnerabilities, and choices that brought a person to court in the first place.

During my years of service, I dealt with cases that were sometimes tragic, sometimes frustrating, sometimes surprisingly hopeful. I saw the devastating effects of addiction, the chaos of untreated mental illness, and the recurring patterns that trap individuals and families in cycles of offending. I also encountered resilience, honesty, and the determination of people who genuinely wanted to change. The courtroom may be a place of consequences, but it is also a place of possibility.

This book is not a collection of sensational tales, nor is it a legal textbook.

It is a reflection on the realities of magistracy the inner workings, the decision-making process, the stories that stay with you, and the human moments that shape your understanding of justice. It is written for those who are curious about what really happens inside the courtroom, for those who care about fairness and public service, and for those who believe, as I do, that justice is at its strongest when balanced with compassion and common sense.

Although every case mentioned has been anonymised and altered to protect identities, the lessons they offer remain true. They illustrate the pressures faced by those who appear in court, the dilemmas faced by those who adjudicate, and the responsibilities we all share in creating safer, more connected communities.

My years as a Magistrate taught me that justice is not merely about rules and penalties. It is about context, behaviour, choices, and the delicate balance between holding people accountable and giving them the opportunity to rebuild. This perspective has guided much of my later work in behavioural change, addiction, mental health, and road safety fields where the law and human behaviour intersect in profound ways.

As you read, I invite you to step with me into the courtroom: to feel the atmosphere, understand the process, and see the person behind each case.

If there is a central message in what follows, it is this: justice is not served by looking only at what someone has done, but by understanding who they are, how they arrived there, and what they need in order to walk a better path.

This is the story of what I learned while balancing justice not just in law, but in life.

Chapter 1 — Becoming a Magistrate: The First Day on the Bench

There are moments in life when a door opens and you step into a world you thought you understood only to discover you were seeing it from the outside all along. My first day as a Magistrate was one of those moments. I had spent years living and working within my community, yet nothing prepared me for the reality of taking my seat on the bench, looking out across a courtroom that suddenly felt larger, quieter, and far more consequential than I had expected.

The morning I first put on the robe, I remember feeling the weight of the responsibility more than the weight of the fabric. Becoming a Magistrate in England and Wales is not an achievement marked by ceremony or grandeur; it is marked by trust.

Ordinary citizens, chosen for their judgement, integrity, and capacity for fairness, are entrusted with the authority to make decisions that can alter the course of a person's life. That trust humbled me then, and it humbles me still.

Walking into court as a new Magistrate felt strangely similar to walking into school as a child. There was a mixture of anticipation and unease, a quiet hope to get things right, and a keen awareness that mistakes even small ones mattered. But unlike the schoolboy I once was, I now carried a duty not to classmates or teachers, but to the public at large. The community was no longer something I was part of; it was something I now served.

The courtroom itself was both familiar and foreign. I had sat in the public gallery before, observing the theatre of justice unfold. But standing behind the bench, I noticed details I had never previously given attention to: the nervous tapping of a defendant's shoe, the subdued murmur of solicitors conferring, the slight tremor in a witness's voice as they took the oath. Every sound seemed amplified, every expression more vivid, every pause heavier with meaning.

I quickly learned that the courtroom is not defined by architecture, but by atmosphere. Justice is not delivered in silence; it is delivered in tension the tension between what happened and what should happen next.

My first case was a simple matter on paper, a routine road traffic offence. Yet the simplicity dissolved the moment the defendant stood before me. He was young, frightened, and visibly overwhelmed exactly the type of individual I had seen hundreds of times in the community, but never from this vantage point. His fear was palpable, and I felt an unexpected surge of empathy. In that moment, I realised that while the law might be written in black and white, its application lived firmly in shades of grey.

I had prepared myself for the procedural aspects sentencing guidelines, admissibility, the structured decision-making process. What I had not prepared for was the humanity of it all. The courtroom was not filled with "offenders" and "wrongdoers"; it was filled with people. People with stories, circumstances, anxieties, and vulnerabilities. People who had made mistakes, people who were overwhelmed by life, people who desperately needed someone to listen as much as someone to judge.

Serving as a Magistrate required me to balance firmness with fairness, authority with humility, and the public interest with the individual in front of me. I quickly learned that good judgement is not merely about applying rules; it is about understanding people. It is about recognising that the person standing before you is often at a crossroads and that your words, tone, and decisions may influence the road they take next.

My first day taught me something essential: justice is not an abstract concept. It is not a distant institution or an intellectual exercise. Justice is lived, moment by moment, in the interactions between those who sit on the bench and those who stand before it. It is a human process, shaped by empathy, grounded in principle, and delivered through the imperfect lens of human experience.

As I left the courthouse that day, I paused on the steps, feeling the cool air wash over me. I realised that although I had been appointed to "administer justice," what I had truly been given was the opportunity to understand my community in a deeper way than ever before. The role was not simply about enforcing the law; it was about engaging with the human condition its fragility, its resilience, and its complexity.

That first day set the tone for every day that followed.

Chapter 2 — Understanding the Courtroom: Ritual, Process, and Purpose

If my first day on the bench taught me the emotional weight of justice, the days that followed taught me its rhythm. Every courtroom has a particular cadence, a mixture of ritual, process, and human unpredictability that shapes the way justice is administered. To the casual observer, proceedings may appear repetitive or procedural.

But from the bench, you quickly come to understand that the courtroom is a living environment ordered, yet deeply human.

The rituals of the court are not mere tradition; they exist for a reason. When the clerk calls the court to order and everyone rises, it is not to elevate the Magistrates, but to elevate the moment. It signals that something important is about to happen. The act of standing creates a pause a breath reminding everyone in the room that decisions made here carry consequences and require respect. Even the simplicity of speaking only when addressed serves to ensure clarity, fairness, and discipline in what can often be emotionally charged situations.

For a new Magistrate, the first challenge is to learn the flow of proceedings. Cases come quickly, often with little time between them. The legal advisors guide you on points of law, ensuring that your decisions remain rooted in statute and precedent. Clerks manage the administration that keeps the courtroom functioning smoothly. Ushers coordinate the movement of defendants, witnesses, and solicitors. It is a carefully balanced ecosystem in which everyone plays a part.

But the formality of the courtroom masks an important truth: behind every title, every role, every ritual, lies a shared purpose to pursue fairness. It is a purpose that anchors the room even when the circumstances of a case feel chaotic.

From the bench, you begin to notice nuances others miss. The atmosphere of the courtroom shifts constantly. You feel the tension when a defendant walks in expecting a prison sentence. You recognise the relief when someone discovers they will retain their driving licence. You sense the frustration of solicitors navigating difficult clients, the stress of police officers giving evidence, the exhaustion of individuals who have been caught in cycles of offending for years.

Some days the courtroom feels heavy. Other days it feels frustratingly repetitive. And then there are moments when an unexpected act of honesty or humility from a defendant breaks through the formality and reminds you why justice matters in the first place.

Understanding the courtroom also means understanding your place within it. As a Magistrate, you are not the protagonist. You are not the storyteller nor the centre of attention. You are the arbiter steady, consistent, and impartial. Your role is not to interrogate or to advocate; it is to listen. To weigh. To question when necessary. To remain calm when emotions run high. And, when required, to deliver outcomes that uphold the law while still acknowledging the humanity of those who appear before you.

The bench is a vantage point unlike any other. From it, you observe the entire sweep of the justice system the pressure on policing, the strain on mental health services, the gaps in social support, the realities of addiction, and the consequences of untreated trauma. These issues do not arrive neatly packaged; they present themselves through the individual standing before you. Each case becomes a snapshot of broader societal challenges, reflected through a single life.

The more time you spend in court, the more you realise that justice is not simply about guilt or innocence. It is about context. A theft may be driven by hunger. A breach of order may stem from untreated psychosis. A road traffic offence may reflect addiction, exhaustion, or panic rather than malice. This does not excuse wrongdoing, but it does shape our understanding of it.

Ritual and process provide the structure. Purpose gives the work meaning. Together, they create a courtroom environment where fairness can be pursued even in the face of complexity.

Each morning when I entered the courtroom, I took a moment to pause before taking my seat. It was a small act of grounding a reminder that although the cases may be numerous and the pace relentless, each person who walked through those doors deserved to be seen, heard, and judged only on the facts before the bench.

Understanding the courtroom was, in many ways, the foundation of understanding justice itself.

And the better I understood that setting its rhythm, its constraints, its pressures, and its quiet humanity the better I became at carrying out my role within it.

Chapter 3 — Authority and Humility: Judging Without Judgement

One of the greatest challenges in becoming a Magistrate is learning to distinguish *judgement* from *judging*. The law requires you to evaluate facts, assess credibility, and impose outcomes. But it never asks you to decide a person's moral worth. That distinction subtle yet profound lies at the very heart of fair justice.

Sitting on the bench confers authority, but authority can be misunderstood. The role is not about superiority, power, or moral certainty. It is about responsibility. It is about ensuring that decisions are made impartially, proportionately, and with an awareness of the life that stands before you. The moment a Magistrate begins to believe they are inherently "above" those who appear in court, the purpose of the role is lost.

I learned early on that humility is not optional in this work; it is essential. The courtroom exposes human frailty on a daily basis. People arrive ashamed, angry, frightened, confused. Some come believing the system is against them. Others come believing the system will protect them. Many come simply overwhelmed by a life that has become unmanageable.

To carry authority in such an environment requires self-awareness. You must be conscious of your tone, your language, your posture, and even your silence. A raised eyebrow, a poorly chosen word, or an assumption left unchallenged can influence a defendant more than the sentence you ultimately impose. Authority, when misapplied, can harm. Authority, when grounded in humility, can clarify, steady, and guide.

There were moments on the bench when I felt the tension between what was legally correct and what felt morally weighty. Sentencing guidelines provide structure, but they cannot account for every nuance and circumstance. A defendant may have committed a serious offence, yet show genuine remorse and a desire to change. Another may have technically committed a minor offence, yet demonstrate a pattern of disregard for responsibility that poses a real risk to others.

Humility allows a Magistrate to see beyond the charge sheet. It enables you to ask questions not to trap or chastise, but to understand. To enquire into context. To explore whether the behaviour is rooted in addiction, desperation, trauma, or something else entirely. These enquiries are not excuses; they are explanations. And explanations matter, because justice without understanding is simply punishment.

During my time on the bench, I was frequently struck by how little separated the individual in front of me from many people outside the courtroom.

A single moment of poor judgement, a stressful life event, a hidden addiction, an untreated mental health condition the line between stability and crisis is thinner than most people realise. Recognising this truth does not diminish accountability; it enhances fairness. It ensures that when you pass sentence, you do so with a full appreciation of the complexity of human behaviour.

True authority in the courtroom is quiet, measured, and confident without arrogance. It does not need to impose itself loudly. It does not rely on intimidation or theatrics. It stems from clarity, consistency, and sincerity. Defendants often told me after hearings even when outcomes were unfavourable that they appreciated being treated with respect. And that respect, more than any fine or sanction, often had the greatest impact on their behaviour.

Humility also means acknowledging your own limitations. Magistrates are not psychologists, social workers, addiction specialists, or mental health practitioners. Yet every day we encounter the consequences of societal gaps in those very areas. Knowing when to seek guidance, when to ask for clarity, and when to lean on the expertise of others is not a weakness. It is a strength of the justice system a safeguard against error.

Over time, I came to believe that "judging without judgement" is not a slogan; it is a discipline. It requires continuous effort, reflection, and a willingness to check your own biases.

It requires remembering that no matter how many cases you hear, each one is new to the person living through it. What is routine to the bench may be life-changing to the defendant.

Authority gives the Magistrate the power to hold individuals accountable. Humility ensures that power is exercised with fairness, empathy, and balance. Together, they form the foundation of justice that is both principled and humane.

This chapter closes a crucial early lesson in magistracy: that the law may be rooted in rules, but justice is rooted in character. And for those entrusted with upholding it, character matters every bit as much as knowledge.

Chapter 4 — The People Behind the Cases

One of the first realisations that settles upon a Magistrate and perhaps one of the most enduring is that no one ever truly expects to find themselves standing in a courtroom. Yet every day, people do. They enter carrying not only the weight of an offence, but the burden of a life story that rarely fits neatly within the confines of a charge sheet. Behind every case, behind every name, behind every quiet shuffle towards the bench, lies a person whose journey is far more complex than the moment that brought them to court.

It is easy, from the outside, to think of defendants as a category "offenders," "wrongdoers," "criminals." These labels are convenient. They simplify. They reassure us that those who appear in court are somehow fundamentally different from the rest of society. But the courtroom quickly dismantles that illusion. Once you sit on the bench, you begin to see patterns, yes but more importantly, you see people. People shaped by circumstance, adversity, fear, loneliness, addiction, or simple human error.

There were individuals who entered the courtroom trembling, visibly terrified. Some had never been in trouble before and were mortified to be there. Others arrived hardened by repeated appearances, resignation etched into their faces. Some were defiant, angry at the world, or frustrated by systems they felt had failed them. Many were vulnerable far more vulnerable than they realised, or than society acknowledged.

I came to understand that the courtroom does not simply hear cases; it reveals lives. The mother overwhelmed by debt who stole food to get her children through the week. The young man who lashed out in a moment of fear. The professional who made a catastrophic lapse in judgement after years of stability. The older gentleman whose life had quietly unravelled beneath the surface. The teenager who followed the wrong crowd because acceptance seemed more valuable than consequence.

Their stories were not excuses, nor were they always relevant to the legal outcome. But they helped me appreciate something fundamental: people rarely end up in court because of one isolated moment. More often, that moment is the tip of an iceberg of struggles, pressures, or unresolved personal battles.

There were those whose lives had been shaped by trauma childhood abuse, foster care, domestic violence. Individuals who had never been given the emotional tools to navigate conflict or adversity. Others carried the invisible weight of mental illness: anxiety so crippling that a court summons felt like a threat to survival; depression so deep that self-care had evaporated; psychosis that made the world a confusing and frightening place.

Then there were the people whose cases stemmed from addiction a recurring presence in the magistrates' courts. Addiction does not announce itself politely. It forces itself into every corner of a person's life, dismantling employment, relationships, health, and self-respect. By the time many individuals stood before us, they were not only dealing with the legal consequences of their actions; they were navigating the wreckage left behind by a dependency they could no longer control.

If I learned anything from my years on the bench, it is that most people do not fall into offending because of inherent criminality. They fall because life, at some point, outpaced their ability to cope.

But amid the hardship, there were moments of extraordinary honesty. Defendants who admitted fault without hesitation. Individuals who expressed genuine remorse. Young people whose eyes filled with tears when confronted with the reality of their actions. Parents who vowed to do better for the sake of their children. People who listened, not because they feared punishment, but because they recognised an opportunity to change.

The stories behind the cases taught me to look beyond behaviour and see the human being beneath. It did not soften the need for accountability the law is the law, and consequences must follow. But it did heighten my awareness that justice, to be meaningful, must acknowledge the complexity of human circumstances.

The bench gave me a vantage point into lives I might never otherwise have encountered. It showed me the resilience of individuals who had endured far more than their offence suggested. It reminded me that compassion is not incompatible with firmness. And it reinforced my belief that when we understand the person behind the case, we deliver justice that is not only lawful but humane.

In the end, the courtroom is not simply a place where cases are adjudicated. It is a place where humanity is revealed sometimes painfully, sometimes unexpectedly, sometimes beautifully. And it is in understanding this humanity that a Magistrate learns to balance justice with perspective, empathy, and truth.

Chapter 5 — Poverty, Desperation, and Survival Crime

One of the most revealing lessons I learned as a Magistrate was that the courtroom often serves as a mirror to society's hidden struggles. Poverty may seldom be discussed openly, but it is written quietly, consistently into the stories of those who appear before the bench. It shapes decisions, narrows choices, and pushes people towards actions they never imagined they would take. And while the law must remain blind to circumstance in determining guilt, it cannot ignore context in determining justice.

Many of the individuals who stood before us were not career criminals or hardened offenders. They were people in crisis. People caught in a tightening loop of financial strain, social exclusion, or emotional exhaustion. People who had reached a point where surviving the week felt more urgent than observing the law.

Theft offences, for example, were often the first indicator of deeper hardship. Shoplifting is easily dismissed as dishonesty or opportunism, but in the courtroom it frequently tells a different story. A mother stealing nappies, formula, or basic food supplies. A pensioner taking toiletries he could no longer afford after a sudden increase in rent or bills. A young man stealing clothing not out of vanity but because he owned so little that he could not maintain his dignity at job interviews.

These were not acts of greed. They were acts of survival.

One case in particular remains with me. A woman in her thirties, shaking with embarrassment, stood before the bench having stolen a pack of children's socks and a loaf of bread. She was mortified. Not defiant, not dismissive mortified. She had fallen into debt after losing her job and was waiting, desperately, for the next support payment. When questioned, she did not attempt to justify her actions. She simply said, "I didn't know what else to do."

Her offence was minor in legal terms, but profound in human ones.

Cases like hers forced me to confront an uncomfortable truth: poverty often criminalises the vulnerable. People who are financially stable rarely face the kinds of pressures that lead to these decisions. Yet for those living week-to-week, one unexpected bill, one missed payment, one broken appliance can trigger a chain reaction that ends in a courtroom.

Fines a common sentence for low-level offences can unintentionally deepen that hardship. Imposing a penalty on someone who is already struggling financially requires careful consideration. You must weigh the law, the guidelines, and the need for deterrence, but also the reality that excessive fines can push an individual further into crisis. The goal is accountability, not ruin.

Beyond theft, poverty also surfaces in offences related to licensing, insurance, and roadworthiness. For some individuals, driving without insurance is not an act of disregard for the law but a reflection of the impossible arithmetic of their lives. They simply cannot afford both rent and a premium. This does not excuse the offence the risks are significant, and the law is clear but it underscores the pressures shaping their decisions.

When poverty intersects with shame, the consequences can be compounded. Many defendants avoided seeking help out of pride. They feared judgement. They believed their value as individuals was tied to their ability to cope independently. By the time they appeared in court, the situation had often deteriorated far beyond the point where early intervention could have helped.

Sitting on the bench, you come to understand that desperation has a logic of its own. It compresses perspective, alters priorities, and distorts risk perception. It leads people to make decisions they know are wrong, even dangerous, but which feel, in that moment, like the only available option.

Poverty-related offending challenges society in ways that punishment alone cannot resolve. The courtroom is not designed to fix housing shortages, insecure employment, benefit delays, or the cost of living. Yet it is often where the consequences of these issues become most visible.

As a Magistrate, your role is not to solve poverty though you may wish you could. It is to recognise its influence, acknowledge its impact, and deliver justice that is proportionate, fair, and grounded in reality rather than assumption. Accountability must remain, but compassion must not be abandoned.

Those who appeared in court because of desperation reminded me of something essential: people rarely commit survival crime because they are uncaring or lawless. They do so because life has squeezed them into corners with no good choices left.

The law protects society. Understanding protects justice.

Chapter 6 — Addiction, Alcohol, and Drug-Driven Offending

If poverty is one of the most visible forces behind offending, addiction is one of the most destructive. During my years on the bench, I came to recognise the unmistakable patterns of lives shaped and often consumed by alcohol and drug dependency. Addiction is not a single issue; it is a storm that tears through every part of a person's existence, leaving chaos in its wake. By the time individuals stand before the court, the legal offence is often only the final, outward symptom of a much deeper struggle.

What struck me most was how addiction blurs the boundaries between choice and compulsion. People often speak of substance misuse as a matter of personal weakness, but the reality is far more complex. Addiction rearranges priorities, rewires reward systems, distorts judgement, and narrows a life until little remains beyond the pursuit of temporary relief. In the courtroom, you do not see "bad people"; you see people whose ability to choose freely has been diminished by a persistent and powerful illness.

Alcohol-related cases were among the most common. Public order offences, assaults fuelled by intoxication, drink driving, breaches of bail or court orders alcohol was woven through it all. Many defendants did not arrive belligerent or defiant; they arrived ashamed. They knew they had crossed a line. They knew the damage they had caused. Some could barely look up from the floor as the charge was read aloud.

I remember one man in particular a father in his forties who had never been in trouble before. He appeared after a drink-driving incident that had, by miracle, harmed no one. He was devastated. Not defensive, not evasive devastated. He told the court plainly, "I was drinking to cope. I didn't realise how bad it had got." That moment of honesty revealed more than any legal document could. His offence was serious, but it emerged from a place of emotional collapse rather than disregard for others.

Drug-driven offending presented its own challenges. Theft to fund dependency, possession charges, assaults triggered by stimulant use, chaotic behaviour linked to withdrawal or bingeing every substance had its pattern. Heroin and other opiates brought individuals whose lives had been stripped to their barest foundations. Cocaine-fuelled cases often involved impulsivity and aggression. Cannabis-related offences, particularly in younger people, were frequently accompanied by anxiety, paranoia, or diminished motivation.

Addiction also coexisted with mental illness at strikingly high rates. Depression masked by alcohol, trauma managed through stimulants, psychosis exacerbated by cannabis or synthetic drugs the courtroom became a crossroads where multiple vulnerabilities collided. It required calmness, clarity, and the humility to acknowledge that not every behavioural issue is a moral failing.

With time, I began to recognise the signs long before the facts were presented. The flat affect, the trembling hands, the lack of eye contact, the agitation, the evasive answers these were not signs of dishonesty but symptoms of someone fighting an internal battle that few could see.

And yet, amid the devastation, there were glimmers of hope. Individuals who arrived determined to turn their lives around. People who embraced detox, counselling, or structured treatment programmes.

Parents who wanted to rebuild relationships with their children. Young men and women who expressed genuine relief at being stopped by police before their dependency escalated further. These were moments that reminded me of the potential for justice not only to punish, but also to interrupt to halt a downward spiral before it became irreversible.

As a Magistrate, you quickly come to understand that addiction cannot be sentenced away. You can impose fines, community orders, disqualifications, or custodial terms, but unless the underlying dependency is addressed, the behaviour is likely to repeat. This is where the justice system often feels stretched asked to solve complex social and health issues using tools designed mainly for deterrence and accountability.

But even within those constraints, the court can provide something valuable: structure. Routine. Expectations. Boundaries. A moment of intervention that forces reflection. Sometimes, that single moment that disruption is what plants the seed of change. In many cases, it is the first time the individual has been forced to stop and confront the scale of their dependency.

My experience in addiction and mental health work helped me see addiction-driven offending for what it was: a human struggle, not a character flaw. Accountability remained essential impaired driving, violent behaviour, and drug-fuelled offending all carry serious risks.

But accountability delivered without understanding is unlikely to change behaviour. It may deter temporarily, but it rarely transforms.

The individuals who appeared before us taught me a profound truth: no one chooses addiction, but everyone deserves the chance to choose recovery. And if the courtroom can help create even the smallest opening for that choice, then justice is being served in its fullest, most humane form.

Chapter 7 — Mental Health in the Justice System

If addiction is one of the most visible forces behind offending, mental health is often the most misunderstood. The courtroom regularly becomes a gateway to the realities of psychological distress a place where individuals in crisis encounter a system designed primarily for legal resolution, not clinical care. For many, their first moment of formal intervention comes not in a GP's office or a mental health service, but in the dock.

Early in my service, I realised that mental health issues rarely announce themselves clearly. They emerge through behaviour erratic, withdrawn, confused, aggressive, incoherent and often during moments when a person's capacity to cope has completely unravelled. What appears, at first glance, to be disrespect, dishonesty, or defiance may, on closer inspection, be fear, disorientation, or complete emotional overload.

Some individuals came before us gripped by anxiety so intense they could barely speak. Others presented with depression so profound that they appeared numb to the proceedings altogether. There were those whose manic energy flooded the courtroom, and those whose psychotic symptoms manifested as paranoia, hallucinations, or agitation. Each case required patience, clarity, and the recognition that what you were witnessing was not wilful behaviour but the visible manifestation of an internal struggle.

I remember a young man who stood trembling as the charge was read. His solicitor explained that he suffered from severe social anxiety; coming into the courtroom had pushed him to the verge of a panic attack. As he tried to answer the simplest of questions, he found himself unable to form words. In that moment, it was clear that the offence itself was almost secondary to the real issue: his mental health was in crisis.

Another case involved a woman whose behaviour seemed erratic and confrontational. At first, it appeared she was simply refusing to cooperate. But as the hearing continued, it became evident that she was in the midst of a mental health episode. Her thoughts were disordered, her responses fragmented. The offence was real, but so was her vulnerability. It was a reminder that mental illness does not choose its moments, nor does it pause for the machinery of the justice system.

These encounters taught me the importance of staying attuned not just to the offence, but to *how* the person presents. A defendant's demeanour can reveal far more than a charge sheet; it can offer crucial insight into their cognitive state, emotional stability, and level of support outside the courtroom.

Yet, despite the prevalence of mental health issues, the justice system is not always equipped to respond adequately. The court can recognise vulnerability, order assessments, or refer individuals to appropriate services but those services are often overstretched. For many defendants, real support lies outside the court's reach, dependent on resources that are inconsistent or insufficient. It creates a situation in which the court must act with sensitivity while still ensuring the law is upheld.

Balancing empathy with legal responsibility can be one of the most challenging aspects of magistracy. Mental health does not absolve someone of responsibility for their actions, but it does shape the context in which those actions occurred. It may influence sentencing options, mitigation, or the need for treatment requirements. It may also explain behaviour that might otherwise be misinterpreted as non-compliance or contempt.

Mental illness also intersects with trauma, homelessness, addiction, domestic violence, and poverty. Many individuals appearing before the bench were dealing with several of these challenges simultaneously.

Their lives had been eroded by factors that went far beyond the immediate offence. Understanding these intersections is crucial to making fair and informed decisions.

Despite the difficulties, there were also moments of hope. Individuals who entered the system in crisis sometimes used the structure of the court process as a turning point. Being faced with the seriousness of their situation often became the catalyst for accepting treatment, engaging with services, or reconnecting with family support. These moments reminded me that justice can serve as an interruption a chance to redirect a life that has spiralled into instability.

My years working in mental health and addiction services taught me something invaluable: behaviour is communication. When individuals act in ways that seem irrational or counterproductive, they are often expressing pain they cannot articulate. Recognising that truth does not undermine justice; it strengthens it. It allows the court to respond in ways that are proportionate, humane, and grounded in understanding rather than assumption.

Mental health cases reinforced, more than anything else, the importance of seeing the person behind the offence. They reminded me that justice is not solely about punishment, but about discernment about understanding *why* something happened, not just *what* happened. And they underscored the reality that, for some individuals, the courtroom is not a place of reckoning but a place of crisis.

As a Magistrate, you learn that you cannot solve the mental health crisis. But you can ensure that those who enter the justice system in distress are treated with dignity, patience, and fairness. You can use your authority to create space for compassion without compromising legal responsibility.

And sometimes, that is enough to make a difference.

Chapter 8 — Road Traffic Cases: Responsibility on the Road

Of all the cases that came before the magistrates' court, road traffic offences were among the most frequent and often the most misunderstood. To some, they appeared minor: speeding, driving without insurance, failing to produce documents, careless manoeuvres, drink driving, drug driving. Yet beneath the surface of these offences lay questions of responsibility, judgement, risk, and behaviour. They offered some of the clearest insights into the way ordinary people can make extraordinary mistakes behind the wheel.

Road traffic cases present a fascinating paradox. Most defendants who appear for these offences are not criminals in the traditional sense. They are everyday people workers, parents, students, tradesmen, professionals who simply made a poor decision.

But that decision, made in seconds, carries consequences measured not only in fines or penalty points but in risk to human life.

Sitting on the bench, I learned that driving offences are far from trivial. A car becomes a two-tonne weapon when handled recklessly or impaired by alcohol, drugs, fatigue, distraction, or arrogance. And yet, many individuals who appeared before us had never stopped to consider this truth. They viewed driving as routine, automatic an extension of their daily life rather than a privilege requiring constant vigilance.

Drink driving was among the most sobering examples. The faces of defendants told their own stories: fear, shame, disbelief, regret. Many insisted they "felt fine" to drive. Others admitted they took a chance, believing they would be safe on a quiet road. Some had convinced themselves that their dependency on alcohol was manageable; others were in outright denial. What united them was the realisation sometimes too late that impairment does not announce itself politely. It clouds judgement subtly, deceptively, and with frightening consequences.

Drug driving, too, became increasingly common. Cannabis, cocaine, prescription medications each substance affected driving behaviour differently. Some users genuinely believed they were safe because they did not feel "high." Others underestimated the lingering effects of the drug, unaware that their reactions, perception, and concentration were compromised.

A few had no insight at all into how their substance use disrupted their ability to control a vehicle. These cases highlighted the growing gap between public perception of drug use and the reality of its impact on road safety.

Then there were the uninsured and unlicensed drivers. Some were brazen, knowingly taking chances. But many were simply overwhelmed by financial pressures or administrative chaos. The excuses were rarely malicious; they were often rooted in anxiety, avoidance, or disorganisation. Yet the consequences were the same. An uninsured driver leaves victims unprotected. A learner driver without supervision places others at risk. Responsibility on the road does not pause for personal circumstances.

Careless and dangerous driving cases offered their own insights. Young drivers, full of confidence but lacking experience, misjudged speed or weather conditions. Exhausted workers pushed through fatigue until their concentration failed. Distracted drivers paid the price for a moment's inattention a text, a phone alert, a lapse in awareness. In each instance, the defendant would say, "It all happened so quickly." And that was precisely the point. Road trauma happens quickly because vehicles move quickly. The decisions behind them must be made with care.

What became clear to me over time was that road traffic cases were rarely about lack of knowledge. Nearly everyone knows the drink-drive limit.

Nearly everyone knows they must insure their vehicle. Nearly everyone knows that speeding or texting behind the wheel can kill. The issue was not awareness it was behaviour. It was the gap between what people *knew* and what they *did* in a moment of stress, temptation, complacency, or flawed judgement.

For many defendants, appearing in court was a profound wake-up call. They realised, sometimes for the first time, that their behaviour had consequences beyond personal inconvenience. They recognised the risk they had posed to their passengers, to pedestrians, to other drivers, and to themselves. Some were grateful for the opportunity to reflect before a tragedy occurred. Others expressed deep remorse because the outcome had already been devastating injuries, damage, or the loss of a licence that their livelihood depended on.

These cases left a lasting impression on me. They reinforced my belief that accountability is not merely punitive; it can be transformative. A fine or disqualification may correct behaviour temporarily, but meaningful change comes from insight from understanding *why* the behaviour occurred and how to prevent it from happening again. This belief later became the foundation of my driving behavioural work. But its roots were planted in the courtroom, case by case, story by story.

If Chapters 1 to 7 revealed the human struggles behind offending, road traffic cases revealed something different:

how ordinary, capable, responsible people can make dangerous decisions without fully realising the risk. They taught me that safe driving is not just a skill, but a mindset. It requires self-awareness, honesty, humility, and respect qualities that not everyone brings to the wheel.

Road traffic cases were not simply administrative matters. They were windows into human behaviour its strengths, its weaknesses, and its blind spots. And they reminded me, again and again, that justice on the road is not about the law alone but about the lives that depend on it.

Chapter 9 — Violence, Anger, and Impulse

Violence in the magistrates' court is often portrayed as deliberate, menacing, or premeditated, but the reality is rarely so simple. Most violent offences that come before the bench are not the calculated acts of hardened criminals. They are acts born of anger, fear, panic, frustration, intoxication, or emotional overload. They reflect not only harm done, but a moment in which someone lost control of themselves and crossed a line they may never have intended to approach.

Violence is a broad spectrum: from pushing and shoving to serious assaults, from neighbour disputes to incidents in pubs or public spaces, from domestic-related offences to confrontations fuelled by alcohol or drugs. What unites many of these cases is their impulsivity.

The majority of individuals who appear before the court for violence do not consider themselves "violent people." Yet, in a moment often less than a minute their behaviour caused injury, fear, or emotional harm.

Anger is one of the most powerful human emotions, and in the courtroom you quickly see how poorly many people are equipped to manage it. Some defendants described feeling overwhelmed by stress, humiliation, or provocation, acting before they had a chance to think. Others admitted that the alcohol or drugs they had consumed stripped away their inhibition, judgement, and emotional regulation. A few carried deep layers of trauma, shame, or unresolved conflict that erupted long before they understood what was happening.

I recall a young man charged with assault after a confrontation outside a nightclub. He had no previous history of violence and appeared utterly devastated by the consequences of a single punch. He told the court, with tears streaming down his face, "I don't know what came over me. It was like I snapped." The CCTV footage suggested exactly that a split-second reaction, disproportionate and dangerous, but clearly impulsive. That moment cost him his clean record, risked his employment, and changed the trajectory of his life.

Domestic-related cases were among the most emotionally charged. These situations were rarely straightforward.

They involved complex dynamics: stress, financial pressure, jealousy, communication breakdown, mental health issues, addiction, coercive control, or long-term relationship strain. The court is not the place to diagnose or untangle these underlying issues, but their presence is undeniable. Offending in these contexts often reflects a pattern of escalating behaviour or, in some cases, a relationship that had reached breaking point.

Anger and violence also emerged in situations where individuals felt cornered or overwhelmed. I remember a man who struck out at a security guard in a shop after being confronted for theft. He later explained that he had been living in temporary accommodation, unemployed and spiralling into depression. When stopped at the door, panic took over. He felt ashamed, frightened, and desperate and in that moment, impulse replaced reason. The incident left him horrified at himself.

These cases taught me that violence is not always driven by intent. It is often driven by emotion unregulated, unmanaged, and uncontrolled. That does not diminish the seriousness of the offence, nor does it absolve responsibility. But understanding the emotional roots of violent behaviour helps the court tailor sentences that protect the public while addressing the factors that led to the incident.

The justice system is designed to deliver proportionate consequences, but it also aims to prevent reoffending.

For many individuals, the most meaningful outcome is not just punishment but intervention: anger management programmes, behavioural work, alcohol treatment, counselling, or structured support. These can transform the impulsivity that led to the offence into insight that prevents future harm.

What became clear to me over time was that violence is rarely about strength. It is about vulnerability vulnerability expressed in destructive, harmful ways. People who resort to violence often feel powerless, threatened, or emotionally overwhelmed. They lack the tools to manage conflict or regulate themselves when tension rises. When their behaviour escalates, the consequences can be life-changing.

But not all cases were bleak. Some individuals showed remarkable remorse and a genuine desire to change. Their shame was not performative; it was visible in their posture, their trembling hands, their broken speech. For those people, the courtroom was not simply a place of punishment but a turning point. It provided the accountability needed to confront longstanding emotional issues they had avoided for years.

The cases involving anger and violence reinforced a truth I observed throughout my time in the magistracy: people's worst moments often come to define them in the justice system, but those moments rarely define who they truly are.

Many defendants were not dangerous individuals; they were individuals who had never learned a safe way to deal with strong emotion.

Violence cannot be excused. But it can be understood. And understanding is what allows justice to respond effectively balancing public safety with the possibility of behavioural change.

In the courtroom, violence teaches us something fundamental about human behaviour: when anger overwhelms judgement, consequences follow. And when justice responds with insight rather than assumption, transformation becomes possible.

Chapter 10 — Youth Offending and the Lost Potential

Youth offending was, without question, one of the most difficult and emotionally complex areas of the magistrates' court. When dealing with adults, you see a lifetime of choices, patterns, and circumstances that have shaped their behaviour. But with young people, you are acutely aware that you are encountering someone at the very beginning of their story. Their future is still unwritten, and yet the choices that bring them to court can mark them long before they truly understand the consequences.

Young offenders were rarely hardened criminals. Most were frightened, confused, embarrassed, or defiant in ways that revealed insecurity rather than confidence.

What struck me most was how often their behaviour reflected not malice, but absence the absence of guidance, support, stability, structure, or opportunity.

When a young person enters the courtroom, the atmosphere changes subtly. You sense the fragility of the situation. You see the anxious glance towards a parent or guardian. You hear the solicitor speak not only about the offence, but about school attendance, home life, peer groups, and emotional wellbeing. It becomes clear, very quickly, that youth offending is seldom the result of a single decision. It is the result of an environment.

Some young people arrived before us after committing impulsive acts: shoplifting with friends, fights at school or in town, reckless behaviour influenced by alcohol, drugs, or peer pressure. Others had been pulled into offending by older individuals who exploited their immaturity. And some perhaps the most tragic cases came from homes marked by instability, violence, addiction, or neglect. They were navigating chaotic childhoods without the guidance or boundaries that many take for granted.

I remember a boy of sixteen who appeared after a public order incident in which he had pushed a security guard. He was small, thin, and visibly terrified. As he stood trembling in the dock, the story became clear: his father had left, his mother struggled with her own difficulties, and he had been drifting between temporary carers and sofa-surfing with friends. His offence was unacceptable, but it was also a symptom of a young life unbalanced and unsupported.

His behaviour was wrong, but he himself was not beyond hope.

In many youth cases, education played a significant role. Young people disengaged from school often found themselves drifting towards risk-taking behaviour. Without routine, structure, or a sense of purpose, it was easy for them to slip into circles where offending felt normal, even inevitable. For some, the possibility of exclusion or academic failure intensified feelings of hopelessness, and offending became an outlet for frustration or a misguided attempt at belonging.

Peer influence loomed large. Few adults appreciate the extent to which young people fear social rejection. For many teenagers, the risk of losing face among friends feels more dangerous than the risk of being caught by the police. That fear drives decisions that defy logic: stealing to impress, fighting to gain respect, drinking to fit in, driving dangerously to appear fearless. It is not wisdom that guides them; it is the desperate need to be accepted.

At the same time, youth offending sometimes emerged from boredom, curiosity, or immaturity. These cases were often the easiest to address, because the behaviour stemmed not from deep-rooted issues but from a lack of foresight and emotional regulation. With the right intervention, these young people could be steered back on track quickly.

But not all cases were simple. There were young people already entangled in intergenerational cycles of disadvantage, addiction, or offending. Their lives had been shaped by instability long before they reached adolescence. The courtroom, for them, became a place where society confronted the gaps it had failed to fill.

In such cases, the court's role extended beyond sentencing. It involved guidance, boundaries, and the opportunity for structured support youth offending teams, restorative justice programmes, counselling, educational pathways, mentoring. These interventions often made the difference between a life diverted and a life derailed.

What became apparent over time was that young people responded profoundly to fairness. They recognised sincerity. They respected consistency. And they listened closely when spoken to with respect rather than condemnation. Many of them had rarely experienced adult authority delivered calmly, clearly, and with genuine interest in their welfare.

I found that the most powerful moments in youth court came not from stern warnings, but from conversations that helped young people see themselves differently. Not as criminals, but as individuals capable of better choices. Capable of change. Capable of building a future that did not mirror their past.

Youth offending cases taught me that potential is fragile. A single mistake can have disproportionate consequences. A lack of support can send a young life spiralling. But with timely intervention, compassion, structure, and accountability, that same life can be redirected.

These young people reminded me that the purpose of justice is not only to correct what has gone wrong, but to protect what could still go right. And for many of the adolescents who appeared before us, the courtroom represented not the end of the road, but a crucial turning point a moment when someone finally said, "Your future is still yours to claim."

Chapter 11 — Repeat Offenders and Breaking the Cycle

Among the many challenges faced in the magistrates' court, few were as complex or emotionally demanding as dealing with repeat offenders. These were individuals who appeared time and again, often for similar offences, their names becoming familiar long before their faces entered the courtroom. Their stories spoke not of isolated mistakes, but of patterns built from struggle, hardship, and behaviours that had become deeply ingrained.

To a first-time observer, it might seem perplexing that someone would repeatedly return to court despite prior sanctions, warnings, or opportunities.

But sitting on the bench, it becomes painfully clear that persistent offending is rarely about defiance alone. It is about cycles of addiction, poverty, trauma, mental health issues, unstable housing, unemployment, or broken family structures. These cycles are difficult to escape, and for some individuals, the justice system becomes part of the rhythm of their lives.

There were defendants whose circumstances seemed trapped in repetition. They would leave the court determined to turn things around, only to be back again months later, apologetic and exhausted. Others appeared resigned, almost detached, as though the process had become routine. A few were combative or despairing, convinced that no one cared and that their situation was unchangeable.

One man I recall vividly had been appearing before the court for years. Low-level theft, breaches of community orders, public order incidents. Each time, his solicitor described the same underlying issues: long-term addiction, homelessness, and untreated trauma. He was articulate and polite in court, but behind his composure was a life marked by instability. His offending was not driven by malice. It was driven by survival, withdrawal, and a profound sense of hopelessness. Until his underlying needs were met, the offending continued not because he wanted to reoffend, but because life offered him no alternatives.

Another woman regularly breached suspended sentences and community orders. Her case file was thick, spanning years of petty theft, fraud linked to addiction, and occasional disorder offences. Yet every time she appeared, she expressed genuine remorse. Her challenge was not a lack of conscience; it was a lack of capacity. When her mental health deteriorated or her addiction escalated, the strategies she used to survive left her vulnerable to reoffending. Without stable treatment, her capacity to comply with orders collapsed.

Repeat offenders often live in constant crisis. They experience pressures that most people cannot imagine the relentless demands of addiction, the instability of insecure housing, the isolation of fractured family relationships, the discouragement of repeated failure. Their lives move from one emergency to the next. Compliance with the law becomes secondary to the immediate need to cope.

This is not to say that persistent offending should be excused. Public safety matters. Victims matter. Communities deserve protection from harm and disruption. But effective justice requires recognising that punishment alone rarely breaks entrenched cycles. If it did, the repeat offenders would not be repeat offenders.

Over time, I came to see repeat offending not as stubbornness but as a symptom of unresolved needs. Many individuals simply lacked the practical tools or emotional resilience required to make sustained change. Without intervention, their behaviour was predictable.

With structured support addiction treatment, mental health services, stable housing, supervision, education, meaningful employment some did manage to break free. And when they did, the transformation was remarkable.

One of the most encouraging moments as a Magistrate came when someone who had been before the court repeatedly finally turned a corner. These occasions were not frequent, but they mattered deeply. The pride in a solicitor's voice, the relief on a defendant's face, the sense of possibility in the room these moments affirmed that change was possible, even for those who had struggled the longest.

Yet these successes also revealed the limitations of the justice system. Courts can impose orders, structure consequences, and encourage engagement with services. But we cannot cure addiction in a hearing room. We cannot resolve decades of trauma during sentencing. We cannot provide the stability that some individuals have never known. The best outcomes often occurred when the justice system, health services, social supports, and community resources aligned something far easier said than done.

Repeat offenders taught me a great deal about human behaviour, particularly the challenges of breaking habits formed under pressure, adversity, or addiction. They reminded me that behaviour is shaped by environment, opportunity, and circumstance.

They reinforced the truth that genuine change takes time, support, and often several attempts.

Most importantly, they showed me that justice cannot focus solely on the offence; it must also consider the person. Not to diminish accountability, but to increase the likelihood that accountability leads to change rather than repetition.

Breaking the cycle of offending is possible, but it requires more than punishment. It requires insight, structure, intervention, and the belief sometimes held only by the court when the individual themselves has lost hope that change is still within reach.

Chapter 12 — The Art of Sentencing: Fairness, Proportionality, Compassion

Sentencing is often portrayed as a simple matter of applying rules: offence committed, penalty imposed. But anyone who has ever sat on the bench knows that sentencing is far from mechanical. It is a deliberative process that requires legal understanding, emotional intelligence, moral clarity, and an unwavering commitment to fairness. It is, in many ways, the most delicate and demanding aspect of magistracy.

Every sentence must balance multiple considerations: the seriousness of the offence, harm caused, culpability, the defendant's circumstances, public protection, deterrence, rehabilitation, remorse, and previous history. These factors rarely point neatly in one direction. Instead, they create a landscape of competing priorities in which the Magistrate must find an outcome that is lawful, proportionate, and just.

One of the first lessons I learned was that sentencing is not about making an example of someone. Nor is it about expressing personal frustration. It is about applying the law with diligence and humility. The guidelines provide structure, but they cannot account for every nuance. Within that structure, the Magistrate must exercise judgement measured, informed, and balanced.

A single case might present a defendant who is remorseful, cooperative, and previously of good character. Another may involve someone who is chaotic, disengaged, or burdened by addiction or mental health issues. The offence might be identical. The sentence rarely is. Justice is not delivered by treating unequal situations equally; it is delivered by treating each case according to its own facts and context.

I remember feeling the weight of sentencing most acutely in cases where the consequences were significant potential custody, disqualification from driving that could cost someone their livelihood, restraining orders affecting families, or community orders requiring intensive supervision. Even decisions on fines, when imposed on someone already living in poverty, carried implications that extended far beyond the courtroom.

There is an art to sentencing because it requires the Magistrate to hold two perspectives simultaneously: the legal framework and the human reality. Too heavy a sentence can crush a person's prospects. Too light a sentence can undermine public confidence and fail to protect victims. The right sentence must sit between these extremes, guided by principle rather than emotion.

Compassion plays an important role, but compassion does not mean leniency. It means understanding. It means recognising the difference between a person who made a single foolish decision and someone whose behaviour poses ongoing risk. It means acknowledging remorse where it is genuine and identifying deflection where it is not. It means giving weight to the challenges a person faces without allowing those challenges to excuse serious harm.

Sentencing is often a conversation with the present, but it is also a statement about the future. Community orders, treatment requirements, rehabilitation programmes, and driving awareness courses all have the potential to influence behaviour beyond the courtroom. When used appropriately, they offer structure and support that punishment alone cannot provide. They help individuals confront the underlying issues that contributed to their offending whether addiction, emotional regulation difficulties, poor decision-making, or lack of insight.

Equally, there are times when the court must impose immediate and firm consequences.

Violence, persistent offending, deliberate harm, and high-risk behaviour require sentences that reflect the seriousness of the actions. The public must be protected. Victims must be acknowledged. Justice must be seen to be done. These decisions are never taken lightly. They demand clarity of thought and the ability to separate personal feelings from legal duty.

What the public often does not see is the emotional toll that sentencing can take. Magistrates are human. There are cases that stay with you sentences that felt necessary but heavy, defendants whose lives were already fractured before the offence, families whose suffering could not be undone. After particularly difficult hearings, it was not uncommon to step out of court needing a moment of stillness to process what had just occurred.

Yet despite the challenges, sentencing is also where justice finds its most meaningful expression. When done well, it demonstrates that the law is not a blunt instrument but a thoughtful framework designed to protect society while offering individuals the opportunity to change. It reassures victims that their experiences matter. It shows defendants that their actions have consequences, but that they also have choices. And it reinforces the principle that fairness is not optional it is the foundation of every decision made on the bench.

Sentencing taught me that justice is both structured and human. It is guided by rules, but delivered with judgement.

It requires firmness, but benefits from compassion. And it demands consistency, but thrives on nuance.

In the courtroom, sentencing is not merely a task. It is an art one that requires the Magistrate to balance duty with understanding, and consequence with possibility. When these elements align, justice becomes not only lawful, but truly fair.

Chapter 13 — When Justice Feels Heavy

There is a quiet truth about life on the bench that few outside the justice system ever fully grasp: justice can feel heavy. The courtroom may be a place of procedure and structure, but it is also a place of emotion raw, unfiltered, and sometimes overwhelming. Every Magistrate carries moments that linger long after the court doors close, moments that stay in the mind and settle on the conscience.

Not every day is difficult, of course. Many hearings are straightforward, and many decisions follow clear guidelines. But woven among the routine cases are those that strike deeper. Cases involving vulnerable individuals, families in crisis, victims carrying invisible wounds, or defendants whose lives seem shaped by tragedy rather than choice. These are the cases that remind you that justice is not abstract. It is personal.

Some of the heaviest moments came from realising that the law, despite its intention and structure, cannot fix everything. You see individuals who desperately need help that extends far beyond what a court can provide support for addiction, mental health treatment, secure housing, or protection from domestic violence. The limitations of the justice system become painfully clear in those moments. You can impose a sentence, but you cannot rebuild a life.

One case that stayed with me involved a young man who had spiralled into addiction after a series of bereavements. He had no prior history of offending, yet within a year, he found himself repeatedly before the court for low-level theft and public order incidents. Each time he appeared, he seemed thinner, more lost, more broken. His solicitor spoke of waiting lists, failed interventions, and the absence of meaningful support. We imposed the most constructive orders available, but every decision felt like placing a plaster on a much deeper wound. Watching someone deteriorate in real time knowing the court could only do so much was one of the most difficult experiences of magistracy.

Domestic cases also carried a particular weight. They revealed the quiet suffering behind closed doors partners living in fear, children caught in conflict, families fractured beyond recognition. You sensed the years of emotional damage long before the incident that brought them to court.

These hearings were often tense, emotionally charged, and laden with complexity. Sentencing in these circumstances required firmness, care, and a keen awareness of the broader impact. Even after delivering a decision, the weight of the situation lingered.

Cases involving young people were perhaps the most affecting. Seeing a teenager standing in the dock frightened, angry, or withdrawn raised questions that remained with me long after the court adjourned. What had this young person experienced? Who had failed them? Could this be a turning point, or was it the start of a long battle with the justice system? You try to steer them towards support and structure, but the uncertainty stays with you.

There were also moments when victims' stories made the weight of the work unmistakable. A victim impact statement delivered through tears, a description of long-term trauma, the lasting effects of violence or intimidation these moments brought into sharp focus the responsibility placed on the bench. Sentencing was no longer an academic exercise. It bore directly on someone's healing, safety, and sense of justice.

Occasionally, despite protocol, emotion found its way into the hearing room. A defendant breaking down when confronted with the reality of their actions. A parent sobbing quietly at the back of the courtroom. A victim struggling to speak.

These were reminders that justice is not merely a system; it is an experience affecting real people with real lives.

Even Magistrates, trained to remain impartial and composed, are not immune to these moments. There were days when the courtroom felt heavy with sadness a succession of cases involving addiction, homelessness, mental illness, or repeated failure. Days when it seemed every story revealed another gap in societal support. Days when the human cost of offending felt overwhelming.

But it is precisely on those days that the role of a Magistrate becomes most important. The responsibility is to remain steady, fair, and humane to provide clarity where there is confusion, boundaries where there is chaos, and structure where there is instability. To ensure that even when justice feels heavy, it is still delivered with integrity.

What sustained me through those moments was the knowledge that fairness matters deeply. Even when the outcomes are difficult, even when the circumstances are tragic, fairness remains the one constant the court can offer. It is the foundation upon which trust in the justice system depends.

Looking back, the weight of certain cases never fully leaves you. But neither do the moments of hope the individuals who turn their lives around, the victims who find closure, the young people who return with gratitude rather than fear, the defendants who reappear months later simply to say, "Thank you, I'm doing better now."

Justice can feel heavy. But it is in carrying that weight with honesty and humility that the work becomes meaningful.

Chapter 14 — When Justice Does Its Job

For all the difficult days in the magistrates' court, for all the cases that weigh heavily long after the courtroom has emptied, there are also days when justice demonstrates its power, purpose, and quiet humanity. These are the moments that remind you why the role matters. They are rarely dramatic. They do not dominate headlines or inspire sensational stories. But they capture the essence of what justice can achieve when fairness, accountability, and opportunity align.

Justice "doing its job" does not mean simply convicting the guilty or imposing firm sentences. It means seeing a genuine change in someone's behaviour. It means witnessing the point at which a person takes responsibility not because the law demands it, but because they themselves recognise the need to do better. It means giving people the structure, clarity, and boundaries they need to step away from chaos and towards a more stable life.

One of the most striking moments came when a young man returned to the court many months after his case had been concluded. He stood at the back of the courtroom, waiting for a quiet moment, and then approached simply to say thank you. He explained that the sentence he received a structured community order with behavioural and educational elements had been the wake-up call he needed. He was working again, had repaired relationships, and was looking to the future with a sense of direction he had never felt before. It was a brief exchange, but it captured the transformational potential of justice delivered with balance.

Another memorable moment involved a woman who had struggled with alcohol-related offences for years. She had been trapped in a cycle of dependency, repeated arrests, and crisis interventions. The court had seen her at her lowest dishevelled, anxious, and consumed by addiction. After finally receiving the right clinical support and engaging in treatment, she returned to court as a changed person. She was sober, stable, and articulate. She spoke honestly about her journey and thanked the court for not giving up on her. It was a reminder that change often requires persistence from the individual and the system alike.

There were also moments in domestic cases where justice meant ensuring safety, clarity, and accountability. A victim expressing relief at being heard.

A defendant acknowledging the impact of their behaviour for the first time. A family given the structure they needed to rebuild or, in some cases, to separate safely. These were not victories in a celebratory sense, but they were vital moments where justice created space for healing and protection.

In road traffic cases, the signs of justice "working" were often subtle but meaningful. A driver determined never to drink or take drugs before driving again. A young motorist who realised the seriousness of careless behaviour on the road. A professional who recognised how stress, fatigue, or distraction had impaired their judgement and resolved to make lasting changes. These moments did not just fulfil the aims of the law; they potentially saved lives.

Sometimes the most powerful outcomes came from restorative processes situations where individuals confronted the consequences of their actions, heard directly from those affected, and expressed sincere remorse. While restorative justice is not suitable for every case, when it works, it can be profoundly impactful. It allows defendants to reconnect with their humanity, and victims to feel recognised rather than forgotten in the legal process.

What I came to appreciate over time was that justice "doing its job" rarely looks like perfection. It rarely provides complete resolution or neat endings. Instead, it offers direction.

It draws boundaries. It helps individuals face uncomfortable truths and take the first steps towards change. It reminds them and sometimes their families that one mistake need not define an entire life.

These moments offered balance to the weight described in the previous chapter. They affirmed my belief that justice is not merely punitive, but transformative. That even small interventions can shift the trajectory of a life. That structure, fairness, and consistency can create stability for those who have never experienced it.

And perhaps most importantly, they demonstrated that human beings are capable of change sometimes dramatic change when they are offered the right support, the right accountability, and the right opportunity.

As a Magistrate, you learn to hold on to these moments. Not sentimentally, but practically. They ground you. They remind you that for all its limitations, the justice system has the power to interrupt destructive behaviour, protect the vulnerable, and help individuals rebuild their lives. These moments are not grand or cinematic, but they are real. And they matter.

Justice does not always cure. It does not always prevent. But when it does its job well, it makes a difference sometimes a quiet difference, but a meaningful one. And it is in these moments that the true purpose of the magistrates' court is revealed.

Chapter 15 — How Magistracy Shaped My Later Work

Serving as a Magistrate did not simply deepen my understanding of the justice system; it reshaped the direction of my entire professional life. The courtroom became more than a place of legal decision-making. It became a classroom a space where patterns of human behaviour revealed themselves with unfiltered clarity. What I witnessed on the bench ultimately guided the path I would take in the years that followed, long after my time in the magistracy came to an end.

Every day in court exposed a truth that no textbook or training session could fully capture: offending is not driven by lawlessness alone. It is driven by stress, trauma, addiction, poor decision-making, emotional dysregulation, lack of support, and the absence of structure or purpose in a person's life. These were not abstract psychological concepts; they were realities played out in front of me, case by case, decision by decision.

It became clear that if society wanted better outcomes fewer victims, fewer broken families, fewer lives derailed we could not rely on punishment alone. We needed to understand behaviour. We needed to understand why people act the way they do, particularly when the stakes are high and the consequences severe. Sitting on the bench reinforced that behaviour is predictable, modifiable, and deeply influenced by circumstance. With the right interventions, people can and do change.

Many of the individuals who passed through the courtroom were not inherently criminal. They were overwhelmed. They were poorly equipped to manage stress, conflict, or emotion. They were struggling with addiction, mental illness, poverty, or fear. They lacked the inner resources to make safe, responsible decisions when it mattered most. And far too often, they had never received the support or education needed to break the cycle.

These observations stayed with me long after I stepped down from the bench. They shaped my belief that effective justice must include a behavioural element an opportunity not just to punish, but to teach, guide, and support change. This belief grew stronger throughout my subsequent work in addiction services, counselling, and mental health. I saw firsthand how understanding behaviour leads to transformation, and how transformation reduces harm.

As the years progressed, everything I had learned from the courtroom the patterns, the triggers, the risk factors, the predictable behaviours began to crystallise. I realised that many of the issues I had seen repeatedly in court were the same issues I was seeing in community settings, in clinics, in coaching sessions, and later in road safety work. Regardless of the context, the underlying drivers were remarkably similar: impulsivity, emotional distress, substance misuse, peer influence, low self-esteem, lack of insight, and poor decision-making.

This convergence of experience ultimately led to the development of behavioural-change programmes, including Drive Aware. Road traffic cases, in particular, highlighted how quickly ordinary people can make dangerous decisions when under the influence of alcohol or drugs, when fatigued, or when emotionally overwhelmed. These were not "criminals" in the traditional sense they were parents, workers, professionals, students. They did not need condemnation. They needed clarity, structure, and practical tools to understand and change their behaviour.

The philosophy behind my later work was rooted in what I learned as a Magistrate:

- Offending is often the outcome of deeper behavioural or emotional issues.

- Insight not fear is what drives real change.

- People respond to fairness, structure, and respect.

- Accountability must be accompanied by understanding.

- Change is possible when individuals are supported, not just punished.

These principles shaped every aspect of the programmes and interventions I developed. They also shaped how I engaged with individuals seeing them not as "offenders," but as people capable of making better choices with the right guidance.

The courtroom taught me that justice is not only about what has happened; it is about what can happen next. It taught me to see potential where others saw problems. It taught me that human behaviour, no matter how entrenched, can shift. And it taught me that meaningful change often begins at the moment someone is held accountable with compassion, clarity, and honesty.

In many ways, the magistracy was the foundation of everything that came after. It gave me the insight to understand behaviour, the perspective to appreciate complexity, and the determination to develop practical, effective ways to support change. It also reinforced a belief I still hold strongly today: that public safety, fairness, and rehabilitation are not competing goals. When approached correctly, they strengthen one another.

The bench shaped me not only as a professional, but as a person. It taught me patience, humility, and open-mindedness. It revealed the human stories behind offending and showed me the power of intervention at the right moment. And above all, it gave me a clear purpose: to use what I had learned to help people make better decisions, protect themselves and others, and break cycles that once felt unbreakable.

Chapter 16 — Reflections on the Future of Justice

Looking back on my years in the magistracy, I am struck by how much the justice system manages to achieve and how much more it could accomplish with the right support, resources, and vision. The court is a place where society confronts its most pressing issues: addiction, mental illness, poverty, trauma, interpersonal conflict, and risky behaviour. Yet it is also a place constrained by time, legislation, and limited intervention pathways. These constraints shape outcomes every day, and they reveal both the strengths and the shortcomings of modern justice.

If the future of justice is to be fair, effective, and humane, it must develop in ways that recognise the complexity of human behaviour rather than relying solely on punishment to control it.

One of the clearest truths I learned on the bench is that offending rarely exists in isolation. Behaviours that lead to court are nearly always connected to deeper struggles: lack of opportunity, emotional distress, stress, addiction, or inadequate support. While the justice system cannot and should not replace social care, health services, education, or community resources, it cannot ignore these factors either. To do so would be to sentence symptoms while leaving causes untouched.

A more holistic justice approach does not mean being lenient or permissive. It means being strategic.

It means aligning the goals of public safety, accountability, and rehabilitation in ways that benefit society as a whole. Prisons and fines may be necessary tools, but they are blunt instruments for addressing entrenched behavioural issues. Community orders, structured programmes, restorative justice, and targeted treatment can often deliver better outcomes for victims, for offenders, and for communities.

One direction the justice system must prioritise is early intervention. Too many individuals arrive in court only after reaching crisis point. By that stage, problems are compounded, harm has been caused, and options are limited. If society invested more heavily in preventative measures mental health services, youth support, addiction treatment, education, employment pathways many offences could be avoided entirely. The justice system would then be used for what it was designed for: accountability, not crisis management.

I also believe that behavioural education must play a greater role in justice. Throughout my later work, I saw how transformative it can be when individuals understand the reasons behind their actions, the risks of their behaviour, and the strategies available to change. Programmes that focus on insight, emotional regulation, decision-making, and accountability can interrupt cycles of offending far more effectively than punishment alone. They equip people with the skills and awareness needed to make better choices long after the court process ends.

Technology and data also have roles to play. Better information sharing between agencies, improved risk assessments, and more efficient case management can ease pressure on courts and allow Magistrates to make more informed decisions. At the same time, we must be careful not to lose the human element. Justice is not a mechanical process; it is a human one. Digital tools can support decision-making, but they cannot replace empathy, intuition, or judicial discretion.

The future of justice must also consider victims more consistently. Their voices matter not only in sentencing, but in understanding the broader impact of offending. Victims often want accountability, but they also want closure, understanding, and reassurance that the person who harmed them will not continue to harm others. A justice system that respects victims must offer clear communication, support, and meaningful opportunities to be heard.

Yet amid all the possibilities for reform, one principle must remain constant: fairness. Fairness is the foundation of the justice system. Without it, public trust erodes, outcomes become inconsistent, and the legitimacy of the courts weakens. Fairness requires impartiality, patience, and the ability to see each case as unique. It also requires humility the recognition that even with guidelines and experience, a Magistrate is making decisions that profoundly impact people's lives.

My hope for the future is a justice system that embraces both accountability and understanding. A system that holds individuals responsible for their actions while recognising the contexts in which those actions occurred. A system that invests in prevention as much as punishment, in rehabilitation as much as deterrence. A system that treats people with dignity, even when imposing consequences. And a system that sees change not as a distant possibility but as a realistic, achievable goal.

The magistracy taught me that justice is a balance a balance between protection and compassion, firmness and perspective, the needs of society and the potential of the individual. The future of justice must preserve that balance while evolving to meet new challenges. It must adapt without losing its integrity, and innovate without abandoning its humanity.

If it can do that, justice will not only serve society; it will strengthen it.

Conclusion — Balancing Justice in a Changing World

As I reflect on my years in the magistracy, I am reminded that justice is not a static institution. It is a living process shaped by people by those who come before the court, by those who support them, and by those entrusted with making decisions on behalf of society.

The courtroom may appear formal and structured, but beneath its rituals lies a complex web of human stories, vulnerabilities, and opportunities for change.

Throughout this book, I have shared the realities of life on the bench: the challenges, the emotional weight, the frustrations, and the moments of hope. I have described the people behind the cases individuals whose lives were often marked by hardship, fear, addiction, trauma, poor judgement, impulsivity, or simple human error. Each one taught me something about behaviour, responsibility, and the fragile line that separates stability from crisis.

If there is a single lesson that stands above all others, it is this: justice is not about perfection. It is about balance. It is the careful and constant effort to weigh harm against context, accountability against compassion, the needs of victims against the potential for rehabilitation. It is recognising the seriousness of offending while understanding the humanity of the offender. And it is delivering consequences that protect society while offering people a chance to change.

Serving as a Magistrate was one of the most meaningful experiences of my life. It sharpened my understanding of human behaviour, strengthened my belief in fairness, and exposed me to the realities of communities under pressure. It also shaped my later work in addiction services, mental health, coaching, behavioural programmes, and ultimately the development of Drive Aware. The insights gained on the bench formed the foundation of the work I do today.

The justice system, like society itself, continues to evolve. New challenges emerge rising mental health needs, increasing substance misuse, social isolation, digital pressures, economic instability. Yet the core principles of justice remain unchanged: fairness, dignity, respect, responsibility, and the belief that people are capable of better when given the right support and structure.

The future of justice will depend on our willingness to see beyond the offence and recognise the person. It will depend on early intervention, behavioural insight, and collaborative systems that address the causes of offending rather than merely its symptoms. It will depend on courts that remain firm, when necessary, compassionate when appropriate, and consistent always.

Most of all, it will depend on remembering that justice is not an abstract system but a human one built on our shared commitment to living safely, respectfully, and responsibly alongside one another.

I hope this book has offered a glimpse into what justice looks like when viewed not from the outside, but from within. I hope it has revealed the complexities, the challenges, and the quiet triumphs of magistracy.

And I hope it has reinforced the idea that justice is not simply a matter for the courts, but a shared responsibility that extends across communities, families, institutions, and individuals.

Balancing justice is an ongoing process one that requires patience, humility, and an open mind. It asks us to hold accountability and compassion in equal measure. And it reminds us that even in difficult circumstances, change is possible.

For every heavy moment in court, there were moments of clarity, learning, and hope. Those moments are what stay with me. They remind me that justice, when applied with fairness and humanity, can make a genuine difference sometimes quietly, sometimes profoundly, but always meaningfully.

This book is dedicated to the people who made those lessons possible: those who appeared before the bench, those who served alongside me, and those who continue to uphold the principles of justice every day. Their stories, their struggles, and their resilience have shaped my understanding of what justice truly is and what it can be.

As society continues to change, the work of justice will remain vital. And with fairness as its foundation, it will continue to protect, guide, and, at its best, transform.